Veg

by Carol Wilson

People choose veganism for a number reasons. As the market for vegan foods increases, many vegan alternatives are now available.

Index

Cover front: Vegan chickpeas burgers with arugula, pickled cucumbers and hummus
Back: Vegan food including tofu, avocado, rice, seedlings and sweet potato
Title page: Vegan selection

Printed & published by Dorrigo, Manchester, England © Copyright

Sweetcorn Potato Chowder

Creamy and hearty, this simple soup is packed with flavour.

**1 tbsp olive oil, 1 onion, chopped
2 cloves garlic, crushed
500g potatoes, unpeeled, cut into chunks
1 litre vegetable stock
440g canned sweetcorn, drained
125ml soya cream, salt and pepper**

**To garnish:
coarsely ground black pepper
1 - 2 tbsp soya cream**

Heat the olive oil in a large pan and cook the onion and garlic for about 5 minutes until soft but not browned. Stir in the potatoes and stock and bring to the boil. Reduce the heat and simmer for 15-20 minutes until the potatoes are tender. Add the corn and soya cream and simmer gently for 5 minutes. Season to taste with salt and pepper. Sprinkle with black pepper and top with a spoonful of soya cream.

Curried Lentil Soup

Spicy and flavoursome and rich in fibre.

**3 tsp curry powder, 3 tbsp olive oil
2 onions, finely chopped, 3 cloves garlic, crushed
20g coriander stalks chopped, thumb-size piece root ginger, grated
300g sweet potatoes, diced, 400g potatoes, diced
1 carrot, diced, salt and freshly ground pepper
1200ml vegetable stock, 100g yellow lentils
300ml soya milk, 1 lime, juice**

**To garnish:
chopped coriander leaves**

Put the curry powder into a large pan, then toast over a medium heat for 2 minutes. Add the olive oil, stirring, then add the onions, garlic, coriander stalks, ginger, sweet potatoes, potatoes and carrots. Season to taste and cook gently for 5 minutes, stirring. Add the stock, lentils, soya milk and a little more seasoning, then cover and simmer for about 20 minutes until the vegetables are tender. Transfer half the soup in batches to a blender or food processor and blend until smooth. Return to the pan and stir in the lime juice. Reheat and ladle into warm serving mugs or bowls. Garnish with chopped coriander.

Soya Bean Salad

Healthy and satisfying for a light lunch.

**400g firm tofu, cubed, 3 - 4 tbsp light soy sauce
3 - 4 tbsp lime juice, 200g soya beans
salt, 1 handful bean sprouts
½ cucumber, thinly sliced
1 - 2 red chillies, sliced, freshly ground pepper
1 - 2 tbsp cornflour , vegetable oil, for deep frying
2 tbsp water, ½ - 1 tsp brown sugar
4 tbsp sesame oil**

**To garnish:
watercress**

Toss the tofu cubes in 2 tablespoons soy sauce and 1 tablespoon lime juice. Cover and chill for 15 minutes. Cook the soya beans in a pan of boiling salted water for about 10 minutes, rinse and drain well. Pat dry the tofu and season well with salt and pepper, then sprinkle with the cornflour. Heat the oil in a large heavy-based pan and cook the tofu for 3-4 minutes. Drain on absorbent kitchen paper. Mix together the remaining soy sauce, lime juice, water and sugar. Season with salt and pepper and stir in the sesame oil. Arrange the salad ingredients and the dressing on serving plates. Place the tofu on top and serve garnished with watercress.

Carrot and Broccoli Pate

A tasty starter, presented in colourful layers.

For the cashew nut layer: 300g raw cashew nuts, soaked overnight in 900ml water
450ml water, 2 tsp soy sauce, 1 tsp cider vinegar, 1 pinch salt

For the broccoli layer: 200g firm tofu, 5 tbsp soya milk, 2 tsp vegan spread
½ tsp salt, ¼ tsp pepper, ¼ tsp Dijon mustard, 4 tbsp lemon juice
1 tbsp ground almonds, 250g cooked broccoli florets

For the carrot layer: 350g cooked carrots
2 tbsp tahini, ½ tsp ground cumin, 1 - 2 tsp olive oil, salt and pepper, to taste

To garnish: bean sprouts, watercress

Line a large terrine dish or loaf tin with cling film. For the broccoli layer: put all the ingredients except the broccoli and almonds into a food processor and blend until smooth and transfer to a bowl. Mash the broccoli with a potato masher and add to the mixture along with the almonds. Mix well and spoon evenly into the dish. For the carrot layer: put all the ingredients into a food processor and blend until smooth. Spoon evenly on top of the broccoli layer. For the cashew nut layer: drain and rinse the soaked cashews well. Put all the ingredients into a food processor and blend until smooth. Put into a large sieve lined with cheesecloth and strain well. Press the cashews with a heavy plate until all the liquid is gone. Spoon the mixture evenly on top of the carrot layer. Cover with cling film and chill overnight. Carefully turn out onto a serving plate and serve in slices. Garnish with bean sprouts and watercress.

Lentil and Vegetable Loaf

Appetising and packed with healthy vegetables, spices, nuts and lentils

**1 tbsp olive oil, 2 tbsp sunflower seeds
100g dry yellow lentils, rinsed, 200g floury potatoes, coarsely grated
2 onions, chopped, 1 clove garlic, chopped
1 leek, chopped, 100g white turnips, chopped
100g pistachio nuts, chopped, 2 - 3 tbsp wholemeal flour
2 tbsp tahini, 2 tbsp freshly chopped parsley
freshly grated nutmeg**

Set the oven to 180°C (160°C fan) gas mark 3. Grease a loaf tin with the oil and scatter with sunflower seeds. Place the lentils in a saucepan and cover with cold water. Bring to the boil, cover and simmer for about 30 minutes until cooked but not disintegrating. Drain and cool. If the potatoes are very wet, squeeze to remove excess liquid. Place in a mixing bowl. Add the onions, garlic, leek, turnip, pistachios, flour, tahini, lentils and parsley to the potatoes and mix well. Season the mixture with salt, pepper and nutmeg and turn into the loaf tin. Smooth the surface and bake for about 40 minutes until golden brown.

Lentil Shepherd's Pie

An excellent winter warmer and perfect for a family dinner.

300g floury potatoes, 2 tbsp vegetable oil
1 onion, finely chopped, 1 carrot, finely chopped
1 red pepper, seeds removed, chopped
1 tbsp flour, 250ml vegetable stock
100g frozen peas, 200g canned green lentils, rinsed and drained
salt and pepper, 75 - 100ml olive oil
freshly grated nutmeg

Set the oven to 200°C (180°C fan) gas mark 6. Grease 4 pie dishes. Cook the potatoes in a pan of boiling salted water for about 25 minutes until soft. Heat the vegetable oil and cook the onions for 5 minutes, then add the carrots and peppers and cook until the vegetables are tender. Dust with the flour and add the vegetable stock. Bring to the boil, stir in the peas and lentils and season with salt and pepper. Drain and mash the potatoes, stir in the olive oil and season with salt, pepper and nutmeg. Spoon the lentil mixture into the dishes and top with mashed potato, smoothing the top and marking with a fork. Bake for about 30 minutes until bubbling and golden brown.

Chickpea Burgers

These mouth-watering burgers are cooked in minutes.

400g canned chickpeas, drained, 200g hazelnuts, chopped
2 onions, grated, 4 carrots, grated
1 red pepper, seeds removed, diced, 1 tsp chopped thyme
1 tbsp tahini, 1 tsp ground cumin, 1 tsp ground coriander
1 tbsp flour, salt and pepper, to taste
4 tbsp vegetable oil

To serve:
vegan bread rolls, split and toasted

To garnish:
salad leaves
cherry tomatoes, halved
onion rings

In a mixing bowl, mash the chickpeas with the other ingredients, except the oil. Shape the mixture into 6-8 burgers and chill for 1 hour. Heat the grill. Place the burgers on the grill pan. Brush with oil and grill for 2-3 minutes until lightly browned. Carefully turn the burgers over, brush with more oil and cook for another 2-3 minutes. Place the burgers on the bread rolls and garnish with salad leaves, cherry tomatoes and onion rings.

Vegetable Biryani

Full of bold Indian flavours, this makes a sumptuous main dish.

400g Basmati rice, 4 tbsp vegetable oil, 2 onions, chopped
1 red pepper, seeds removed, cut into strips
3 tsp grated root ginger, 2 cloves garlic, finely chopped
1 cinnamon stick, broken, 6 cardamom pods, lightly crushed
1 ½ tsp ground cumin, ¼ tsp chilli powder
½ tsp turmeric, ½ tsp saffron threads
675ml vegetable stock, 175g green beans, trimmed
200g baby corn cobs, halved, 1 tsp salt
75g cashew nuts, 75g almonds, chopped

Rinse the rice in several changes of water to remove the excess starch, then soak in a bowl of cold water for 30 minutes. Drain well. Heat the oil in a large pan and cook the onions and pepper strips for about 5 minutes until soft and starting to colour. Add the ginger and garlic and cook for 2 minutes. Stir in the spices and rice and cook for 1 minute until fragrant and the rice is coated. Add the stock, green beans, corn cobs and salt and bring to the boil. Cover and simmer gently for about 10-15 minutes until the liquid is absorbed and the vegetables are just tender, but still crisp. Leave to stand, covered, for 10 minutes until the rice is tender. Heat the remaining oil in a frying pan and cook the cashews and almonds until lightly browned. Remove the cinnamon stick from the biryani and stir in the nuts. Serve on warm serving plates.

Stir-fried Tofu with Sweet and Sour Vegetables

Delicious and quick and simple to cook

For the marinade: 3 tbsp sesame oil
1 tbsp dark soy sauce, 2 tbsp rice syrup
2 cloves garlic, crushed, 600g firm tofu, cubed

For the stir-fry: 3 tbsp sunflower oil
4 spring onions, finely chopped, 2 cloves garlic, finely chopped
1 red chilli pepper, seeds removed, finely chopped,1 red pepper, seeds removed ,finely chopped
1 cucumber, peeled, seeds removed, chopped, 2 small tins pineapple chunks, drained
3 tbsp dark soy sauce, 2 tbsp vinegar
salt and pepper

Stir together the ingredients for the marinade in a bowl, add the tofu and mix well. Set aside for 2 hours. For the stir-fry: heat the oil in a wok and stir-fry the spring onions, garlic and chilli pepper. Add the red pepper and cook for 5 minutes, stirring all the time. Add the cucumber, pineapple chunks and the remaining ingredients, cook for 2 more minutes, then season to taste with salt and pepper and serve immediately.

Cabbage Roulades with Quinoa

Quinoa is a grain packed with protein, fibre, vitamins and minerals.

**250g quinoa, 500ml boiling water, 1 clove garlic, crushed
2 - 3 tbsp grated vegan cheese, 100g ground almonds
1 - 2 tbsp finely chopped parsley, salt
freshly ground pepper, 8 medium-sized cabbage leaves
2 tbsp olive oil, for frying, 250ml vegetable stock**

Put the quinoa, boiling water and a pinch of salt into a bowl. Stir and cover and leave to stand for 15 minutes to swell. Drain well. Set the oven to 180°C (160° fan) gas mark 4. Add the garlic, cheese, almonds and parsley to the quinoa and season with salt and pepper. Blanch the   cabbage leaves for 3-4 minutes in a pan of boiling salted water. Then remove, rinse thoroughly and pat dry with kitchen paper. Cut away the thick leaf stalks and spread the leaves flat. Divide the quinoa mixture between the cabbage leaves and roll up to form parcels. Tie with kitchen string. Heat the oil in a roasting tin and quickly fry the rolls for 1-2 minutes on each side. Pour in the stock, cover and cook in the oven for about 25 minutes. Serve hot.

Vegetable Fritters with Tomato Yoghurt Dip

These crisp golden fritters are a great way to use up left over vegetables.

110g self-raising flour
1 tsp soya flour
55ml water, 1 tsp salt, 1 tbsp chopped parsley
400g potatoes, grated, 1 carrot, grated
1 courgette, grated, 125g asparagus, chopped ,
1 onion, finely chopped
1 tbsp chopped sun-dried tomatoes
vegetable oil, for deep frying

To serve:
225g soya yoghurt
225g sun-dried tomatoes in oil, drained and chopped

Beat together the flours, water and salt in a mixing bowl until smooth and thick. Stir in the parsley and vegetables. Heat the oil in a fat fryer or deep heavy-based pan and fry spoonfuls of the mixture in batches until crisp and golden. Drain on absorbent kitchen paper. To serve: Place the yoghurt and sun-dried tomatoes in the bowl of a food processor. Blend until smooth. Add salt and pepper to taste and put into a serving bowl. Serve the fritters with the dip.

Squash Stew with Pesto Dumplings

Aromatic dumplings make this hearty casserole even more comforting.

1 tbsp olive oil, 1 onion, chopped
½ tsp salt, ½ tsp freshly ground black pepper
1 bay leaf, ½ tsp dried thyme
450g canned chopped tomatoes, 900ml vegetable stock
50g pearl barley, 1 butternut squash, cubed
1 small sweet potato, cubed

For the dumplings:
200g self-raising flour, plus extra for rolling
100g shredded vegetarian suet, salt and pepper
2 tbsp vegan pesto, water

Heat the oil in a pan and cook the onion for 5 minutes until softened. Add the salt, pepper, bay leaf, thyme, tomatoes, and stock. Bring to the boil and stir in the barley. Reduce the heat, cover and simmer for 30 minutes. For the dumplings: mix the flour and suet in a mixing bowl. Season with salt and pepper. Stir in the pesto and just enough water to form a soft dough. Roll into small balls with floured hands. Set aside. Add the squash and sweet potato to the pan and return to the boil. Add the dumplings, reduce the heat, cover and simmer for about 20 minutes until the vegetables are tender and the dumplings are risen and cooked through.

Red Thai Curry with Tofu and Vegetables

A fragrant curry that's quick to make.

**300g long grain rice, 600ml water
salt, 2 tbsp sesame oil, 600g firm tofu, diced
2 red peppers, seeds removed, cut into strips
1 onion, finely sliced, 1 ½ cm root ginger, peeled and finely chopped
1 clove garlic, finely chopped, 1 ½ tbsp red curry paste
6 kaffir lime leaves, halved, 450ml coconut milk
1 ripe mango, peeled and cut into bite-sized pieces, lime juice**

Put the rice in a pan with the water and salt and bring to the boil. Cover and simmer until the rice is cooked and the water is absorbed. Heat the oil in a wok and brown the tofu on all sides. Remove the tofu and set aside. Add the peppers, onion, ginger and garlic to the wok and cook gently until softened. Stir in the curry paste, add the lime leaves and cook briefly. Add the coconut milk and simmer for 5-7 minutes. Stir in the tofu and mango and season to taste with lime juice. Serve with the cooked rice.

Vegetable Paella

A flavoursome vegan version of the classic Spanish dish.

**2 ½ tbsp olive oil, 2 cloves garlic, crushed
1 large onion, finely chopped, 1 stick celery, finely chopped
2 firm tomatoes, peeled and chopped, 100ml boiling water
½ tsp saffron threads, 300 g Calasparra or paella rice, rinsed and drained
1 tsp paprika, 700 - 800ml vegetable stock
1 large carrot, diced, 225g green beans, trimmed chopped into 1cm lengths
1 red pepper, seeds removed, diced, 150g peas
salt and pepper, 180g black olives, pitted**

Heat 2 tablespoons olive oil in a paella pan or large frying pan. Add the garlic and cook for 1 minute, then add the onions and celery. Cook gently until softened, then add the tomatoes and cook for 5 minutes. Add the saffron to the boiling water and stir well, then add to the pan and simmer for 3 minutes. Add the rinsed rice to the pan with the paprika, stock and saffron water and saffron threads. Bring to a simmer and cook for 10 minutes. Stir the mixture and add the chopped carrots, green beans, and red pepper. Cook for 20 minutes, then stir in the peas and continue cooking, stirring occasionally, until the rice is tender and the stock absorbed. Add a little more stock or water if the mixture is too dry. Season to taste with salt and pepper and stir in the olives.

Vegetable Ragout with Sweet Potato Topping

Colourful and tasty, this is a perfect winter dish.

**3 large sweet potatoes, cut into chunks, 250g puy lentils, rinsed
500ml vegetable stock, 1 tbsp vegetable oil
2 large carrots, chopped, 2 sticks celery, chopped
½ onion, chopped, 2 cloves garlic
400g canned mixed beans, drained
250g canned chopped tomatoes, 50 - 75ml olive oil
2 tsp tomato puree, 2 tbsp red wine
salt and pepper to taste**

Set the oven to 200°C (180C° fan) gas mark 6. Grease a baking dish. Cook the sweet potatoes in a pan of boiling salted water for about 20 minutes until tender. Put the lentils in a pan with the vegetable stock. Bring to the boil, cover and simmer for 15 minutes. Heat the vegetable oil in a pan and cook the carrots, celery, onions and garlic for 5 minutes. Add the beans, tomatoes, tomato puree and wine and bring to the boil. Add the lentils and simmer for 20 minutes until tender, adding water if required. Season to taste with salt and pepper. Put into the baking dish. Drain the sweet potatoes and mash with olive oil, salt and pepper, until smooth. Spread the mashed sweet potatoes on top of the vegetable mixture. Cook for 30-40 minutes, until the topping is browned.

Vegetable Pizza

You can top this pizza with grated vegan cheese if you wish

For the base: 300g strong bread flour, plus extra for kneading
1 tsp fast-action dried yeast, 1 tsp salt, 200ml warm water, 1 tbsp olive oil

For the topping:, olive oil, 1 yellow pepper, seeds removed, cut into strips
1 onion, chopped, 1 aubergine, thinly sliced
1 courgette, sliced, 1 tbsp semolina, 400g canned chopped tomatoes, drained in a sieve
2 tbsp tomato puree, salt and freshly ground black pepper, 1 tbsp dried oregano,
8 - 10 black olives

To garnish: rocket

For the base: mix together the flour, yeast and salt in a mixing bowl. Make a well in the centre and pour in the water and oil. Mix to a soft, fairly wet dough. Turn onto a lightly floured surface and knead for 5 minutes until smooth. Put into a lightly greased bowl, cover with a tea towel and leave to rise until doubled in size - about 1 hour. Set the oven to 200°C (180° fan) gas mark 6. Line a baking tray with non-stick baking paper. Quickly knead the dough and roll out into a large round about 25cm in diameter. Place on the baking tray. For the topping: heat 1 tablespoon of oil in a frying pan and cook the pepper and onion until softened but not browned. Heat the grill. Brush the aubergine and courgette slices with olive oil. Grill on both sides until lightly browned. Brush the dough with a little olive oil and sprinkle with the semolina. Mix together the tomatoes and tomato puree. Season to taste with salt and black pepper. Spread over the base of the dough. Sprinkle with half the oregano. Arrange the vegetables and olives on the dough and sprinkle with the remaining oregano. Drizzle lightly with oil. Bake for about 20 minutes until golden and bubbling. Garnish with rocket.

Spicy Moroccan Vegetable Tagine

Ras-el-hanout is a classic spice mixture used in Moroccan cuisine and contains more than 20 different spices.

**250ml vegetable stock, few saffron threads
1 medium butternut squash, peeled and cubed, 2 carrots, chopped
1 red pepper, seeds removed, chopped, 1 large potato, cubed
75g ready to eat dried apricots, chopped, 100g green beans
400g canned chickpeas, drained, salt and pepper
2 tbsp vegetable oil, 2 onions, finely chopped
2 cloves garlic, finely chopped, 1 ½ tsp ground cumin
½ tsp ground cinnamon, ½ tsp ground coriander
1 tsp ras el hanout spice mixture, 1 tsp smoked paprika
¼ tsp chilli flakes, 1 tbsp tomato puree, 400g canned chopped tomatoes**

To serve: Soya yoghurt

Heat the oil in a large pan and gently cook the onions for 5-8 minutes until softened and caramelised. Add the garlic and continue to cook for 2 minutes. Add the spices and chilli flakes and cook for 2 minutes. Add the tomato puree and cook for a further 2 minutes. Add the tomatoes, stock, saffron, butternut squash, carrots, pepper and potatoes to the pan. The liquid should only just cover the vegetables. Stir well and simmer for 5 minutes. Add the apricots, green beans and chickpeas and continue to cook for a further 10 minutes until all the vegetables are tender. Season with salt and pepper. Serve with a spoonful of yoghurt.

Coconut and Lime Ice Cream

A refreshing, creamy ice cream. Make sure the can of coconut milk doesn't contain stabilisers

150ml water
115g caster sugar
2 limes
400ml canned coconut milk

Put the water and sugar in a pan and stir. Heat, stirring constantly until the sugar has dissolved completely. Remove from the heat, leave to cool, then chill well. Grate the lime zest into the chilled syrup and stir in the lime juice. Add the coconut milk. Put into an ice cream maker and churn until firm enough to scoop. Alternatively, pour the mixture into a freezerproof container and freeze for 5-6 hours, beating twice with a fork or whisk during the freezing time, to break up the ice crystals.

Banana Ice Cream

You can add some chopped walnuts or pecans after the final whisking, if you wish.

4 ripe bananas
300ml coconut or soya cream
55g caster sugar

Mash the bananas in a bowl or food processor until very smooth. Whisk in the cream and continue whisking until blended and air bubbles appear. Whisk in the sugar until well blended. Put into a freezerproof container, cover and freeze for 2 hours. Whisk until any frozen lumps are smoothed out and return to the freezer for another 8-10 hours, whisking every few hours to prevent ice crystals from forming. Allow to stand at room temperature for a few minutes before serving.

Strawberry and Lychee Sorbet

Light and refreshing, this is completely fat free.

110g caster sugar
225ml lychee syrup, from the can
1120g canned lychees in syrup, drained
500g strawberries, chopped
½ lemon, juice

Heat the sugar in the lychee syrup in a pan over a low heat until the sugar has dissolved completely. Set aside to cool. In a food processor or blender, blend the strawberries and lychees until smooth. Mix together the strawberry/lychee mixture, lemon juice and syrup mixture. Pour the mixture into an ice cream maker and churn according to the manufacturer's instructions until firm. Alternatively place the mixture in a freezerproof container and freeze for 30 minutes. Beat with a fork or whisk, to break up the ice crystals. Freeze for a further 20 minutes. Repeat the beating twice more during freezing until the mixture is completely frozen. Serve in scoops.

Vanilla Cupcakes

Deliciously light and topped with a creamy frosting.

275g self-raising flour
1 tsp baking powder
225g caster sugar, 200ml sunflower oil
200ml sweetened soya milk
1 tsp vanilla extract

For the topping:
400g icing sugar, 150g sunflower margarine
2 tsp vanilla extract

Set the oven to 180°C C (160° fan) gas mark 4. Place paper cases in a 12 hole deep bun tin. Mix the flour, baking powder and sugar together in a large bowl. Make a well in the centre and add the sunflower oil, soya milk and vanilla. Use a large metal whisk to thoroughly combine all the ingredients. Spoon the mixture into the paper cases and bake for 18–20 minutes, until well risen and firm to the touch. Leave to cool in the tin for at least 1 hour before adding the   topping. For the topping, sift the icing sugar into a large bowl and add the margarine and vanilla. Beat well until smooth and creamy. Spread the topping on the cooled cupcakes or spoon into a large piping bag and pipe on top. Chill for 30–60 minutes to set before serving.

Bran Muffins

Wholesome and healthy, these are perfect for elevenses or afternoon tea.

175g wholemeal flour, 175g light muscovado sugar
110ml sunflower oil, 4 tbsp wheat germ
4 tbsp oat bran, 4 tbsp wheat bran
2 tsp baking powder, 225ml water
2 tbsp black treacle , 1 tsp vanilla extract
1 ½ tsp cider vinegar, 75g raisins or sultanas

Set the oven to 180°C (160° fan) gas mark 4. Place 8 paper cases in muffin tins. Put all the dry ingredients into a mixing bowl and stir to combine. Mix together the water, treacle and vanilla. Add to the dry ingredients with the oil and vinegar and mix slowly until thick. Stir in the raisins. Pour into the paper cases and bake for 15-20 minutes until golden. Cool on a wire rack.

Carrot Cake with Coconut Cream Frosting

Make sure the can of coconut milk doesn't contain stabilisers

340g plain flour, 1 tsp baking powder
1 tsp bicarbonate of soda, ½ tsp salt
1 tsp ground cinnamon, 3 carrots, finely grated
175ml apple juice, 110ml sunflower oil
100ml agave syrup, 110g caster sugar
1 unwaxed orange, finely grated zest
For the frosting:, 400g can coconut milk, chilled overnight
140g icing sugar, 1 tsp vanilla bean paste

For the cake: set the oven to 170°C (150° fan) gas mark 3. Grease a 23cm cake tin and line the base with non-stick baking paper. Mix together the flours, baking powder, bicarbonate of soda, salt and cinnamon in a mixing bowl. Stir in the carrots. Whisk together the apple juice, oil, agave syrup, sugar and orange zest. Gently stir into the flour mixture. Pour into the tin and bake for 50-60 minutes, until a skewer inserted into the centre comes out clean. Cool in the tin for 10 minutes, then turn out onto a wire rack to cool completely. For the frosting: open the can of coconut milk upside down and pour off the thin liquid. Scoop the thick coconut milk into a large bowl, sift in the icing sugar and add the vanilla. Whisk for 2-3 minutes until soft and fluffy. Spread the whipped cream on top of the cold cake. Chill until ready to serve.

Fresh Orange Upside Down Cake

Moist and bursting with flavour, a perfect tea time treat.

200ml water, 175g granulated sugar
1 - 2 unwaxed oranges, very thinly sliced
180g plain flour, 225g caster sugar
1 tsp bicarbonate of soda
½ tsp salt, 225ml orange juice
75ml sunflower oil, 1 tbsp white vinegar
1 tsp vanilla extract

Heat the water and sugar in a pan over a low heat until the sugar has dissolved completely. Add the orange slices and bring to the boil. Reduce the heat, cover and simmer for about 20 minutes, until the oranges are tender. Set the oven to 180°C (160° fan) gas mark 4. Grease a 20cm cake tin. Press the orange slices into the base of the tin, overlapping them slightly. Spoon over a little of the cooking syrup. Put the flour, caster sugar bicarbonate of soda and salt into a mixing bowl and stir to combine. Whisk together the orange juice, oil, vinegar and vanilla until smooth. Whisk into the dry ingredients. Pour into the tin and bake for 30-35 minutes until golden and cooked through. Test by inserting a skewer or cocktail stick into the centre of the cake - if it comes out clean the cake is cooked. Remove from the oven and leave to cool in the tin for 10-15 minutes. Turn the cake out so that the orange slices are uppermost.

Fruit Cake

This vegan version of an old traditional recipe is easy to make.

200g caster sugar, 2 tbsp sunflower oil
½ tsp ground cinnamon, ½ tsp freshly grated nutmeg
½ tsp mixed spice, ½ tsp salt
175g mixed raisins, currants, sultanas
350ml water, 250g plain flour
1 tsp baking powder
1 tsp bicarbonate of soda

Lightly grease a 20cm round cake tin or 23cm square cake tin. Mix together the sugar, oil, cinnamon, nutmeg, mixed spice, salt, raisin mixture and water in a pan over a medium heat Bring to the boil and continue boiling for 5 minutes. Remove from the heat and leave to cool. Set the oven to 180°C (160° fan) gas mark 4. Sift the flour, baking powder and bicarbonate of soda together. Add the flour mixture to the cooled fruit mixture. Stir until just combined. Put into the tin. Bake for 20-25 minutes until cooked through and browned. Cool in the tin for 10 minutes, then turn out onto a wire rack to cool completely.

Chocolate Banana Cake

If you love bananas and chocolate, this cake is for you!

250g plain flour, 100g caster sugar
2 tbsp soya flour, 3 tsp baking powder
3 - 4 tbsp cocoa powder
250ml soya milk, 80ml sunflower oil
4 tbsp water, 2 ripe bananas, chopped

Set the oven to 180°C (160° fan) gas mark 4. Grease a loaf tin. Put all the dry ingredients into a large bowl and mix together. Mix all the wet ingredients in a separate bowl, then quickly mix into the dry ingredients. Fold the bananas into the mixture. Spoon into the tin and bake for 30-40 minutes (test to see if it is done by inserting a cocktail stick or skewer, which should come out clean). Cool in the tin for a few minutes, then turn out onto a wire rack to cool completely.

Chocolate Truffle Cake

A crisp biscuit base topped with velvety smooth rich chocolate truffle. Lotus biscuits are vegan and available from supermarkets.

200g Lotus caramelised biscuits, crushed to crumbs
80g vegan margarine, melted
450g vegan plain dark chocolate, 70% cocoa solids
5 tbsp liquid glucose
2 tbsp rum, brandy or orange juice,
250ml soya cream

To decorate: cocoa powder

Grease a 23cm cake tin and line the base with non-stick baking paper. Mix the crushed biscuits with the melted margarine and press into the base of the tin. Press down with the back of a spoon. Chill while you make the filling. Melt the chocolate, glucose and rum in a heatproof bowl placed over a pan of simmering (not boiling) water. Remove from the heat, cool slightly and gently stir in the soya cream. Pour into the tin onto the biscuit base and chill overnight. Place on a large serving plate and sift cocoa powder over the top.

Meringues

Light, airy, sweet meringues made with aquafaba (liquid from canned chickpeas).

6 tbsp liquid from a can of chickpeas
1/4 tsp cream of tartar
100g granulated sugar
½ tsp vanilla extract

Place the chickpea liquid and cream of tartar a large bowl. Using an electric whisk, start at a slow speed and whisk until foamy. Gradually increase the speed until the mixture is white and glossy and stiff peaks start to form. Slowly add the sugar, whisking all the time at high speed. Whisk in the vanilla, whisking until glossy, stiff peaks form. Set the oven to 120°C, (100° fan) gas mark ½ . Line a baking tray with non-stick. baking paper. Pipe or spoon the meringue mixture into small shapes onto the tray. Place in the oven and bake for 45 minutes. After 45 minutes, switch off the oven, but don't open. Leave the oven off, but don't open it for one hour. Store the cold meringues in an airtight container in the 'fridge for up to 5 days.

Blueberry Pancakes

These light, fluffy pancakes are easy to make.

240g self-raising flour
15g sugar
1 pinch salt
340ml almond milk
30ml sunflower oil, plus extra for cooking
100g blueberries

Put the flour, sugar, salt, almond milk and oil into a bowl and whisk to a smooth batter. Add the blueberries and stir through. Heat a non-stick frying pan over a medium heat and lightly brush with oil. add 2 tablespoons batter to the pan at a time to make small, round pancakes. You will need to do this in batches. Cook for 3-4 minutes until the edges are set, and bubbles appear on the surface. Flip the pancakes over and cook for another 2-3 minutes until golden on both sides and cooked through. Keep warm in a low oven while you cook the remaining pancakes.

Shortbread Biscuits

Delightfully crumbly sweet golden biscuits.

100g vegan margarine
75g caster sugar, plus extra for sprinkling
1 pinch salt
175g plain flour
100g rice flour

Cream the margarine, sugar and salt in a mixing bowl until light. Stir in the flours. Bring the mixture together in your hands and knead lightly for a few moments until smooth, but avoid over handling. Wrap the dough in cling film and flatten into a disc. Chill for 1 hour until firm. Set the oven to 170°C (150° fan) gas mark 3. Line a baking tray with non-stick baking paper. Roll out the dough between 2 sheets of non-stick baking paper, about 5mm thick. Use a cookie cutter to cut into shapes, then place the shapes on the tray well-spaced to allow for expansion. Prick the tops with a fork and sprinkle with sugar. Bake for about 20-25 minutes until pale golden brown. Cool on the trays for 10 minutes, then place on a wire rack to cool completely.

Muesli Bars

These bars are a great lunch box treat. Use walnuts or macadamia nuts as a variation.

110g sunflower margarine
85g light muscovado sugar
85g golden syrup
275g high fruit muesli
75g chopped nuts, cashews, almonds, etc.
3 - 4 tbsp sesame seeds

Set the oven to 180°C (160° fan) gas mark 4. Line a 23cm x 32cm baking tin with non-stick baking paper. Heat the margarine, sugar and golden syrup in a pan until just melted. Add the muesli and nuts and mix well. Tip into the baking tin and spread evenly. Sprinkle with sesame seeds. Bake for 15-20 minutes until golden. Mark into 12 bars and leave to cool completely in the tin, as it falls apart when warm. Cut when cold.

No Bake Green Tea Fridge Cake

Matcha is a vibrant green tea powder made from the highest quality Japanese tea leaves.

225ml melted coconut oil
225ml agave syrup, 675g raw cashew nuts, soaked overnight
175ml lemon juice, 1 ½ tbsp matcha green tea powder, more if needed
1 unwaxed lemon, finely grated zest
1 pinch salt, 200g vegan plain biscuits, crushed
175g roasted hazelnuts, chopped
170g vegan margarine, melted

Line a 900g loaf tin with a double layer of cling film. Mix together the coconut oil and agave syrup. Put the well- drained cashews, lemon juice, matcha powder, lemon zest, salt and the oil/agave mixture into a food processor. Blend until very smooth. Add more matcha for a stronger matcha flavour. Spread a thin layer on the sides and base of the tin. Chill for 30 minutes. Mix together the biscuits, nuts and margarine. Sprinkle about 1/3 over the chilled matcha layer base. Add another layer of the matcha mixture and repeat the layers, ending with the matcha mixture. Chill for at least 4 hours until set. Alternatively freeze for about 2 hours. Cut into slices to serve.

Spanish Churros with Chocolate Dip

*Churros are golden, crisply fried pastries, often dusted with sugar and ground cinnamon.
Here, they're served with a luxurious chocolate dip.*

For the churros:
225ml water
2 ½ tbsp sugar
½ tsp salt
few drops vanilla extract
110g plain flour
sunflower oil, for deep frying

For the dip:
175g vegan plain dark chocolate, 70% cocoa solids, chopped
110ml rice or soya milk
1 tsp vegan margarine

For the churros: put the water, sugar and salt into a pan and bring to the boil, stirring. Remove from the heat, add the flour all at once and the vanilla and beat until smooth. Heat the oil in a deep fat fryer or deep heavy-based pan. Spoon the churros mixture into a piping bag fitted with a fluted nozzle. Pipe 7.5cm lengths of dough directly into the hot oil and cook for 3-4 minutes until golden, turning once. Do this in batches as it is important not to overcrowd the pan. Drain on absorbent kitchen paper. For the dip: put all the ingredients into a pan and heat very gently until the chocolate has melted. Stir and serve with the churros.

Chocolate Lemon Truffles

A deliciously fruity truffle with lemon that cuts through the sweetness of the white chocolate.

100g vegan white chocolate
100g vegan milk chocolate, 30% cocoa solids
1 unwaxed lemon, finely grated zest
50ml soya cream, 50g coconut oil
100g cocoa powder

Melt both the chocolates in a large heatproof bowl over a pan of simmering (not boiling) water. Cool slightly. Stir in the lemon zest, soya cream and coconut oil and mix until smooth. Cover and chill for 2 hours. Sift the cocoa powder onto a plate. Roll teaspoons of the mixture into small balls between your hands. Roll in the cocoa and put onto a plate. Chill for 1 hour before serving.

Metric Conversions

The weights, measures and oven temperatures used in the preceeding recipes can be easily converted to their metric equivalants. The conversions listed below are only approximate, having been rounded up or down as may be appropriate.

Weights

Avoirdupois	Metric
1oz	Just under 30 grams
4oz (1/4 lb)	approx. 115 grams
8oz (1/2 lb)	approx. 230 grams
1lb	454 grams

Liquid Measures

Imperial	Metric
1 tablespoon (liquid only)	20 millilitres
1 fl. oz	approx. 30 millilitres
1 gill (1/4 pt)	approx. 145 millilitres
1/2 pt	approx. 258 millilitres
1 pt	approx. 570 millilitres
1 qt	approx. 1.140 litres

Oven Temperatures

°Fahrenheit		Gas Mark	°Celsius
Slow	300	2	150
	325	3	170
Moderate	350	4	180
	375	5	190
	400	6	200
Hot	425	7	220
	450	8	230
	475	9	240

Flour as specified in these recipes refers to plain flour unless otherwise described.